irresistible
sorbets
sherbets, water ices
& granitas

sara lewis

irresistible
sorbets
sherbets, water ices
& granitas

LORENZ BOOKS

First published by Lorenz Books in 2002

© Anness Publishing Limited 2002

Lorenz Books is an imprint of Anness Publishing Limited
Hermes House, 88-89 Blackfriars Road, London SE1 8HA

Published in the USA by Lorenz Books
Anness Publishing Inc.
27 West 20th Street, New York, NY 10011
www.lorenzbooks.com

This edition distributed in Canada by General Publishing
895 Don Mills Road, 400–402 Park Centre,
Toronto, Ontario M3C 1W3

A CIP catalogue for this book is available from the
British Library.

PUBLISHER Joanna Lorenz
MANAGING EDITOR Linda Fraser
SENIOR EDITOR Margaret Malone
DESIGNER Adelle Morris
STYLIST Penny Markham
FOOD STYLIST AND ADDITIONAL RECIPES
   Joanna Farrow
COPY EDITORS Rosie Hankin and Jenni Fleetwood
EDITORIAL READER Joy Wotton
PRODUCTION CONTROLLER Claire Rae

10 9 8 7 6 5 4 3 2 1

NOTES Bracketed terms are intended for American readers. For all recipes, quantities
are given in both metric and imperial measures and, where appropriate, measures
are also given in standard cups and spoons. Follow one set, but not a mixture,
because they are not interchangeable. Standard spoon and cup measures are level.
1 tsp = 5ml, 1 tbsp = 15ml, 1 cup = 250ml | 8fl oz.
Australian standard tablespoons are 20ml. Australian readers should use 3 tsp in
place of 1 tbsp for measuring small quantities of sugar, spice, etc.
Medium (US large) eggs are used unless otherwise stated.
The very young, the elderly, pregnant women and those in ill-health or with
a compromised immune system are advised against consuming raw eggs or dishes
and drinks containing raw eggs.

contents

Sorbets and similar iced desserts are the classic choice for refreshment on a hot summer's afternoon or for a light and elegant finish to a meal. They may no longer be the sumptuous perfumed creations that graced the tables of the aristocracy of the 18th century, but they are every bit as popular.

Frozen desserts have come a long way since the Romans scooped up snow and flavoured it with honey and fruit, or Chinese lords supped on iced syrups scented with flowers. Turks and Arabs favoured iced drinks made from milk or cream, called *chorbet* or *charab*. These came to the attention of the wider world when the trade routes opened up in the early 13th century, and as techniques for freezing improved, they evolved into softly frozen desserts.

Sorbets, sherbets, water ices and granitas are all similar, but there are a few fundamental differences. Sherbets come closest to the original iced drinks, and continue to be based on milk or cream, but sorbets are more refreshing mixtures, consisting of fruit purées and syrups, with whisked egg white added to lighten the mixture. Water ices do not contain egg white, so they are denser and more intensely flavoured. Flowers or spices may be infused in the syrup, and a fruit flavouring is often enhanced with a complementary wine or liqueur. Italian granitas consist largely of water, with flavouring and some sugar to prevent them from freezing too hard. Unlike water ices, which are churned to smooth silkiness, the granita mixture is frozen, then beaten at regular intervals to create a crunchy crystalline mass, like frosted snow.

Most iced desserts are very easy to make, whether you have an ice cream maker or not. Make them as bold and vibrant as you like, by utilizing seasonal fruit and herbs and adding a dash of liqueur for extra flavour, or stick to the classics such as lemon sorbet and coffee granita for guaranteed elegance. Add a pretty flower as decoration, and you have a delightfully easy dessert.

introduction

equipment for ices

Making sorbets and similar desserts is easy. You'll probably find everything you need in your kitchen or pantry. If you've got the time, you can make ices by hand and freeze them in tubs, but they will need to be whisked frequently while freezing. Save time and effort by using an ice cream maker.

PARING CITRUS RIND

ELECTRIC WHISK

GETTING STARTED

The basic ingredients of all iced desserts are a sugar syrup and a fruit purée or other flavouring. A heavy pan is essential for making the syrup and cooking the fruit and you will need a sieve for puréeing.

For preparing citrus rind, a cannelle knife, zester or vegetable peeler will be invaluable, as will a grater and a lemon squeezer. If you intend to make sorbets, sherbets or water ices by hand, you will need plastic tubs or similar freezerproof containers. A granita must freeze as fast as possible, so use a stainless steel roasting pan or shallow cake tin (pan) for that purpose.

An electric whisk makes short work of breaking down ice crystals in frozen desserts, or you can use a food processor, if you prefer.

ICE CREAM MAKERS

These appliances work by churning the ice dessert mixture constantly while it freezes. The most efficient ice cream makers have their own freezing units, and stand on the worktop. They have two bowls – a stainless steel one that is built in and a separate aluminium bucket that is slotted into the larger, fixed bowl. Most machines of this type have a see-through lid for easy viewing,

plus a vent for pouring in additional ingredients. The only drawbacks with this type of ice cream maker are size (they are larger than a food processor, so they take up quite a bit of storage space) and noise. Motors do vary, so try to see – and hear – the machine in operation before you buy.

A cheaper alternative is an ice cream maker that features a detachable double-skinned bowl. In the wall cavity is a liquid that becomes extremely cold when frozen. Before use, the bowl must be placed in a freezer for 18 hours at the very least. It is then removed, fitted with a lid that includes paddles and connected to the electricity supply. The

ICE CREAM MAKER

SMALL METAL MOULDS

ICE CREAM SCOOPS

MELON BALLER

EQUIPMENT FOR STORING AND SERVING

It is useful to have a selection of tubs for storing ice cream in the freezer. When filling tubs, leave a headspace of 2cm | ¾ in to allow for increased volume after freezing. Lids should fit snugly to eliminate the transfer of strong smells and flavours. It is vital to label tubs clearly – it's only too easy to confuse pumpkin soup with mango sorbet at a later date.

The colder the freezer, the more quickly the mixture will freeze, making for smaller ice crystals and a smoother result. If the freezer is badly packed the motor will have to work harder to maintain temperature. The optimum temperature is -18°C | -65°F.

There are a number of ice cream scoops available. Choose from stainless steel cup half-moon shaped scoops with sleek steel handles, simple spoon scoops with metal or easy-grip moulded plastic handles, or efficient metal and brightly coloured plastic scoops with quick release levers. To be really impressive, use silver spoons.

Sorbets and sherbets look elegant when scooped with a melon baller. They are available from good cookshops and usually have a grape-size cup at one end and a pea-size cup at the other.

machine is switched on and the chilled mixture is poured in. The paddles turn until the mixture is thick enough to scoop, a process that takes about half an hour. If your freezer is large enough to house the bowl permanently, this type is ideal for impromptu ices, but it can be irritating if you want to make a sorbet and have to wait until the next day while the container chills.

Whatever type of ice cream maker you use, follow the manufacturer's instructions carefully.

MOULDS

Because they melt more quickly than ice cream, sorbets and similar desserts are not often moulded, but mixtures can be frozen in small metal moulds or iced lolly (popsicle) moulds.

ingredients and flavourings

Iced desserts don't demand elaborate ingredients. All are based on a syrup made by dissolving sugar in hot water in a pan, and you don't get much simpler than that. Egg white is sometimes added to lighten the mixture, and flavourings vary from fruits to flowers, spices, chocolate, coffee and spirits.

ADDING SUGAR

SUGAR SYRUP

Making a sugar syrup is done by simply mixing sugar and water in a heavy pan and heating it until the sugar dissolves. Caster (superfine) sugar is often used, because it dissolves quickly, but soft brown sugar, granulated sugar or even honey also work well. The syrup can be flavoured with pared citrus rind, ginger, chilli or lavender. Once made, the syrup can be stored in the refrigerator for several days.

WHISKED EGG WHITE

EGG WHITE

Adding egg white to a sorbet not only lightens the mixture, but also helps to stabilize it, which is important for those sorbets that melt quickly. There's no need to beat the egg white; a quick whisk with a fork is all that is required.

FRUIT

Tart citrus fruit such as lemons, limes and grapefruits make crisp, refreshing sorbets. Sweet oranges and clementines are often partnered with a spirit such as tequila or vodka.

For a boldly flavoured (and coloured) dessert, berries are an excellent choice. Choose mixed red berries, blueberries or raspberries. Cranberries will give a subtle flavour, as will strawberries, especially when mixed with lavender.

Certain fruit partnerships are old favourites. Try pears with white wine, apples with a splash of dry cider or gooseberries and elderflowers. Plums and peaches also work well. For more unusual iced desserts, experiment with the various melons. Watermelon granita is superb as is iced melon sorbet frozen in a cantaloupe melon shell. Kiwi fruits also make a softly coloured iced dessert.

Fruit is usually puréed in a sugar syrup to give a smooth texture.

BLUEBERRIES

EDIBLE FLOWERS AND FLORAL ESSENCES

The addition of an edible flower or essence can add depth and subtlety to a dessert, and make the perfect decoration, as well. Lavender is especially good in a strawberry sorbet, while elderflowers lend their subtle fragrance and taste to gooseberry ices. Rose water is a luxurious touch, and its presence can be signalled through the sprinkling of a few rose petals over the finished dessert.

SPICES

Fire meets ice when warm spices are used to make frozen desserts. Mixed (apple pie) spice, cinnamon and cloves are ideal in ices that accompany rich meals, while star anise adds a bold liquorice-like flavour and aroma. Ginger is particularly good with kiwi fruit, and when chilli is combined with citrus such as lemon and lime, the result is an unusual and exciting water ice.

CHOCOLATE AND COFFEE

Two more ingredients that contribute warm flavours are chocolate and coffee. For both, choose good quality products to ensure a really good, strong flavour, such as Belgian chocolate and freshly ground espresso coffee beans.

WINE, CIDER AND SPIRITS

Both red and white wine are used in iced desserts, as is cider. Liqueurs such as Cointreau and Grand Marnier are also popular, but it is important to add only the quantity recommended in the recipe, as too much alcohol will inhibit the dessert from freezing.

MAKING FRUIT PURÉES

berry fruits Purée in a food processor or blender until smooth, then press the purée through a sieve into a bowl, using the back of a spoon. Discard any seeds remaining in the sieve.

apples and pears Peel, core and slice, then poach in a little syrup until tender. Process to a smooth purée. Pear purée can be flavoured with white wine, brandy and lemon juice, while the flavour of apples is enhanced if a little cider is added.

peaches and plums These can be puréed raw if they are fully ripe, then sieved to remove the skins. Damsons are a bit fiddly to prepare, so poach them first in syrup, then either scoop out the stones or sieve the purée.

melons These are puréed raw. Cut in half, skin, then scoop out as many seeds as possible. Remove the rest by sieving the purée.

making a basic sorbet

Sorbets are made with a simple sugar syrup, which may be flavoured, and then stabilized and lightened with whisked egg white. This basic method – without the egg white – is used for water ices. Sherbets are made in a similar way, but with milk, cream or fromage frais instead of fruit juice or purée.

STEP 2

STEP 3

STEP 6

1 Put the sugar and water in a pan and gently heat the mixture, stirring until the sugar has just dissolved.

2 Flavour the syrup by adding pared citrus rinds, spices such as cinnamon sticks or cloves, or edible flowers. Leave to cool and infuse.

3 If you are making a fruit sorbet, purée the fruit in a food processor, then rub it through a sieve into a bowl to remove any skins or seeds. It may be necessary to cook some types of fruit first.

4 Stir the purée or other additional flavouring into the cool syrup. Add any other ingredients specified in the recipe, such as liqueur. Chill the mixture in the refrigerator. The colder it is, the quicker it will freeze later.

5 Strain the mixture, if necessary, then transfer it to an ice cream maker and churn until it is fairly thick, but still too soft to scoop. This may take up to 40 minutes, depending on your machine. If you are making the sorbet by hand, freeze it in a plastic tub or similar freezerproof container for 4 hours until mushy.

6 Lightly whisk the egg white with a fork until just frothy. If you've used an ice cream maker, just add the egg white and continue to churn until the sorbet is thick enough to scoop. If the mixture was frozen in a tub, soften it by beating it until smooth with a fork or electric whisk or by whizzing it in a food processor or blender. Beat in the whisked egg white and return the sorbet to the tub. Freeze for 4 hours, or until firm.

QUANTITIES A total of 750ml | 1¼ pints | 3 cups liquid will provide six small portions of sorbet. As an approximate guide, 500g | 1¼lb | 5 cups of berry fruits or ripe, stoned and chopped peaches, plums or nectarines will produce about 450ml | ³/₄ pint | scant 2 cups purée. Mix this with 150–200g | 5–7oz | ½–1 cup sugar that has been dissolved in 300ml | ½ pint | 1¼ cups water. Stir in the juice of ½ lemon. The quantity of the sugar needed will vary according to the sweetness of the fruit you are using. Add 1 egg white and any extra flavouring.

making a basic granita

What distinguishes granitas from other iced desserts is their grainy texture; the result of being beaten rather than churned. The classic granita is based on sweetened black coffee, but there are also chocolate and fruit versions. Whatever the mixture, all are frozen in the same way.

STEP 1

1 To make a coffee granita, pour hot coffee into a shallow plastic tub or a roasting pan to a depth of no more than 2–2.5cm | ³/₄–1in. Add sugar and stir to dissolve it in the hot liquid. Leave to cool, then freeze the mixture in the coldest part of the freezer for 2 hours until it is mushy around the edges.

2 Take the container out of the freezer and beat the granita well with a fork to break up the ice crystals. Return the granita to the freezer. Beat it at 30-minute intervals for 2 hours more until it has the texture of snow.

QUANTITIES A total of 1 litre | 1³/₄ pints | 4 cups liquid will provide six portions of granita. Use strong black coffee, sweetened with 150g | 5oz | ²/₃ cup caster sugar.

STEP 2

OTHER FLAVOURINGS
citrus juice Grate the rind from unwaxed fruit, then squeeze the juice. Make a syrup by heating 115–200g | 4–7oz | ¹/₂–1 cup sugar and 300ml | ¹/₂ pint | 1¹/₄ cups water in a pan to dissolve the sugar. Allow to cool, then stir in the juice and half the rind from 6 oranges or lemons, or 4 ruby grapefruit. Top up with water, if necessary, to make up to about 1 litre | 1³/₄ pints | 4 cups.
berry purée Purée 500g | 4oz | 3¹/₂ cups fruit in a food processor or blender, then press through a sieve to remove the seeds. Make a simple syrup using the above amounts of sugar and water. Cool, transfer to a container, then add the berry purée and juice of 1 lemon, and stir well. Top up with water to make up to 1 litre | 1³/₄ pints | 4 cups. Chill, then freeze.

CITRUS JUICE

BERRY PURÉE

serving iced desserts

Impress your friends at your next dinner party by trying one of the following serving suggestions. They are not difficult to achieve, but look stunningly professional. Complete the effect with beautifully simple citrus curls and frosted flowers scattered on top, or use pretty fresh fruit, flowers and herbs.

MAKING TINY SCOOPS

PIPING SHAPES

SCOOPS AND SHAVINGS
Ices can be formed into various shapes; for best results allow ices to soften slightly before shaping. Dip the scoop into warm water before using, and rinse between scoops.

rounds These are easy to make if you use a proper ice cream scoop. Dip it into warm water, then press it along the surface of the ice until a well rounded shape has been formed. Rinse the scoop in warm water before continuing. In the same way, use a melon baller when you want tiny scoops.

ovals Quenelles are made by using two dessertspoons. Scoop up sorbet or sherbet with one spoon, then invert the other on top to shape it to a neat oval. Use the second spoon to slide the ice off.

shavings Pare off long, curved shavings by pressing a spoon into an iced dessert and dragging it at an angle of 45 degrees.

MAKING PIPED SHAPES
Whirls of sorbet can be piped straight on to serving plates or into fruit cases or chocolate moulds. Use a large piping (pastry) bag fitted with a cream nozzle. Sorbets and sherbets may need to be set slightly with gelatine before piping and freezing. Dissolve 15ml | 1 tbsp powdered gelatine in a little water, stir into the sugar syrup, then proceed as usual.

USING CITRUS SHELLS
Colourful fruit shells look very pretty filled with sorbet or other ice mixtures. Cut the top off lemons, limes, oranges or clementines. Loosen the edges of the flesh with a sharp knife, then carefully scoop it into a bowl, leaving the shells intact. Rinse and drain the shells well, then pipe or spoon a little of the ice into each of them. Replace the lids, wrap in clear film (plastic wrap) and freeze until needed. Garnish with a fresh herb sprig. Use the citrus flesh in the sorbet. Cut grooves in the skin of the fruit with a cannelle knife (zester), if you wish.

CITRUS SERVING CUPS

MAKING AN ICE BOWL

Many iced desserts look spectacular when served in a pretty ice bowl. The ice bowl can be decorated with small flowers, slices of citrus fruit or herbs and spices such as bay leaves and star anise.

Ice bowls are easy to make – just make sure there is enough room in your freezer. You will need two toughened glass or plastic bowls, one about 2.5cm | 1in larger in diameter than the other. Add a few pieces of crushed ice to hold up the inner bowl, then tape them together, so that the gap between the bowls is the same all the way round. Fill the gap with cooled boiled water, then carefully slide your chosen decorations into the water, teasing them into position with a long skewer. Freeze overnight until solid.

To unmould, peel off the tape. Place the bowls in a washing up bowl half filled with hot water. Pour a little hot water into the smaller bowl. Count to 30, then lift the bowls out of the water, pour the water out of the smaller bowl and loosen the ice bowl with a thin, round-bladed knife. Lift out the inner bowl, turn out the ice bowl and put it on a plate. Lightly strew the plate with flowers and fill the ice bowl with scoops of sorbet, sherbet or water ice.

USING MOULDS

Dense mixtures can be frozen in cups or glasses that have been lined with clear film (plastic wrap). To turn out, dip the mould into hot water, invert on to a plate, then lift off the mould.

QUICK DECORATIONS

frosted flowers Brush a little egg white over pansies, rose buds or violas, sprinkle with caster (superfine) sugar and leave on a wire rack to dry. Use on the day of making.

sugared lemon rind Using a cannelle knife (zester), thinly pare the rind of a lime, orange or lemon to form citrus curls. Dust the curls with a little caster sugar before using.

citrus peel corkscrews Use a cannelle knife to pare long, narrow strips of citrus rind. Twist each in turn around a cocktail stick (toothpick) so that they form corkscrews. Slide the sticks out and hang the curls over the edges of glasses.

sorbets and sherbets

Satin-smooth sorbets and sherbets are the perfect finish to all sorts of meals, from *al fresco* summer barbecues to stylish dinner-party menus. They can be served between courses, to cleanse and refresh the palate, and they are also ideal eaten just as they are on a sunny afternoon. Sorbets and sherbets couldn't be easier to make, and pleasure lies in their simple elegance. For a stylish and contemporary dessert, try lavender sorbet or a slice of iced melon with a splash of Pimm's, or for a bold burst of flavour serve red berry sorbet.

lemon sorbet

INGREDIENTS

200g | 7oz | scant 1 cup
caster (superfine) sugar

300ml | ½ pint | 1¼ cups
water

4 lemons

1 egg white

sugared lemon rind,
to decorate

SERVES SIX

STEP 1

STEP 2

STEP 3

This is the absolute classic sorbet. Refreshingly tangy and yet deliciously smooth, it quite literally melts in the mouth. Dust the lemon rind in a little caster sugar for an easy but delightful finishing touch.

1 Put the sugar and water into a pan and heat, stirring occasionally, until the sugar has completely dissolved, then bring to the boil. Remove from the heat and, using a vegetable peeler, pare the rind thinly from two of the lemons so that it falls straight into the pan of syrup. Simmer for 2 minutes without stirring, then take the pan off the heat. Leave to cool, then chill.

2 Squeeze the juice from all the lemons and add it to the syrup. Strain the mixture into an ice cream maker and churn until thick. If you are making the sorbet by hand, freeze it in a plastic tub or similar freezerproof container for 4 hours, or until it is mushy.

3 Lightly whisk the egg white with a fork until just frothy. If you've used an ice cream maker, just add the egg white and continue to churn until thick enough to scoop. If the mixture was frozen in a tub, soften the mixture by whizzing it in a food processor, then beat in the whisked egg white and return the sorbet to the tub. Freeze for 4 hours, or until firm.

4 To serve, scoop into bowls or glasses and decorate with the sugared lemon rind.

COOK'S TIP Cut one-third off the top of a lemon and retain it as a lid. Squeeze the juice out of the larger portion. Remove any membrane and use the shell as a ready-made container. Scoop or pipe sorbet into the shell, top with the lid and add lemon leaves or small bay leaves. Serve on a bed of crushed ice, allowing one lemon per person.

VARIATIONS Sorbet can be made from any citrus fruit. As a guide you will need 300ml | ½ pint | 1¼ cups fresh fruit juice and the pared rind of half the squeezed fruits. Use four oranges or two oranges and two lemons, or, for a grapefruit sorbet, use the rind of one ruby grapefruit and the juice of two. For lime sorbet, combine the rind of three limes with the juice of six. Use unwaxed fruit or scrub before paring. When using oranges, you will need only 150g | 5oz | ⅔ cup sugar.

pear and sauternes sorbet

Based on a traditional sorbet that would have been served between savoury courses, this fruity ice is delicately flavoured with the honeyed bouquet of Sauternes wine, and spiked with brandy.

STEP 1

1 Peel, quarter and core the pears. Thinly slice them into a pan and add the sugar and 60ml|4 tbsp of the measured water. Cover and simmer for about 10 minutes, or until the pears are just tender.

2 Tip the pears and the water into a food processor and process until smooth, then spoon into a bowl. Leave to cool completely, then chill. Stir the wine, brandy and lemon juice into the chilled pear purée with the remaining water.

3 Transfer the mixture to an ice cream maker and churn until thick. If you are making the sorbet by hand, freeze the mixture in a plastic tub or similar freezerproof container for 4 hours, or until it is mushy.

4 Lightly whisk the egg white with a fork until just frothy. If you've used an ice cream maker, just add the egg white to the churned mixture and continue to churn until thick enough to scoop. If the mixture was frozen in a tub, soften it by whizzing it in a food processor, then beat in the egg white and return the sorbet to the tub. Freeze for 4 hours, or until firm.

5 Serve the sorbet in small dessert glasses, with a little extra Sauternes poured over each portion. Decorate with the sugared mint sprigs.

COOK'S TIP Sorbets that contain alcohol tend to take a long time to freeze, especially when made in an ice cream maker. To save time, transfer the sorbet to a tub as soon as it thickens and finish freezing it in the freezer.

INGREDIENTS

675g|1½lb ripe pears

50g|2oz|¼ cup caster (superfine) sugar

250ml|8fl oz|1 cup water plus 60ml|4 tbsp extra

250ml|8fl oz|1 cup Sauternes wine, plus extra to serve

30ml|2 tbsp brandy

juice of ½ lemon

1 egg white

fresh mint sprigs, dusted with icing (confectioners') sugar, to decorate

SERVES SIX

strawberry and lavender sorbet

There is something very enjoyable about using fresh herbs and flowers in cooking. This delightful pastel pink sorbet is delicately perfumed with just a hint of lavender and is perfect for a special-occasion dinner.

STEP 2

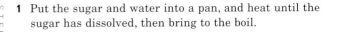

STEP 4

1   Put the sugar and water into a pan, and heat until the sugar has dissolved, then bring to the boil.

2   Take the pan off the heat, add the lavender flowers and leave to infuse (steep) for 1 hour. If time permits, chill the syrup before using.

3   Purée the strawberries in a food processor or in batches in a blender, then press the purée through a large sieve into a bowl.

INGREDIENTS

150g | 5oz | ²/₃ cup caster (superfine) sugar

300ml | ¹/₂ pint | 1¹/₄ cups water

6 fresh lavender flowers, plus extra to decorate

500g | 1¹/₄lb | 5 cups strawberries, hulled

1 egg white

SERVES SIX

4   Transfer the strawberry purée to an ice cream maker and strain in the lavender syrup, then churn until thick. If you are making the sorbet by hand, mix the strained syrup and purée in a plastic tub or similar freezerproof container and freeze for 4 hours until mushy.

5   Lightly whisk the egg white with a fork until just frothy. If you've used an ice cream maker, just add the egg white and continue to churn until thick enough to scoop. If the mixture was frozen in a tub, soften it by whizzing it in a blender or food processor, then beat in the whisked egg white and return the sorbet to the tub. Freeze for 4 hours or until firm.

6   Serve the sorbet in scoops, piled into tall glasses, and decorate with a few sprigs of lavender flowers.

COOK'S TIP If the lavender flowers are very small you may need to use eight. To double check, taste a little of the cooled lavender syrup. If you think the flavour is a little mild, add two or three more flowers, reheat and cool again before using.

red berry sorbet

INGREDIENTS

150g | 5oz | ²/₃ cup caster (superfine) sugar

200ml | 7fl oz | scant 1 cup water

500g | 1¹/₄lb | 5 cups mixed ripe berries, hulled

juice of ¹/₂ lemon

1 egg white

small strawberries and strawberry leaves and flowers, to decorate

SERVES SIX

This vibrant red sorbet seems to capture the true flavour of summer. Pick your own berries, if you can, and use them as soon as possible. For extra flavour, add a dash of vodka or cassis, if you like.

1 Put the sugar and water into a pan and heat gently, stirring until the sugar has dissolved. Bring to the boil, then pour into a bowl, leave to cool, then chill.

2 Purée the fruits in a food processor or blender, then press through a sieve into a large bowl. Stir in the syrup and lemon juice.

3 Transfer the berry mixture to an ice cream maker and churn until thick. If you are making the sorbet by hand, freeze the mixture in a plastic tub or similar freezerproof container for 4 hours, or until mushy.

4 Lightly whisk the egg white with a fork until just frothy. If you've used an ice cream maker, just add the egg white and continue to churn until thick enough to scoop. If the mixture was frozen in a tub, soften it by whizzing it in a food processor or blender, then gently beat in the whisked egg white and return the sorbet to the tub. Freeze for 4 hours, or until firm.

5 Scoop the sorbet on to plates or into bowls, and decorate with a few whole and halved fresh strawberries, as well as the leaves and flowers.

COOK'S TIP Use a mixture of berries for the best flavour, using at least two different kinds. Choose from strawberries, raspberries, tayberries and loganberries.

blackcurrant sorbet

Wonderfully sharp and bursting with flavour, this is a very popular sorbet. If you find it a bit tart, add a little more sugar before freezing.

1 Put the blackcurrants in a pan and add 150ml| ¼ pint|⅔ cup of the measured water. Cover the pan and simmer for 5 minutes, or until the fruit is soft. Cool, then purée in a food processor or blender.

2 Set a large sieve over a bowl, pour the purée into the sieve, then press it through the mesh with the back of a spoon. Pour the remaining measured water into the clean pan.

3 Add the sugar and heat gently, stirring until the sugar has dissolved. Bring to the boil, then pour the syrup into a bowl. Cool, then chill. Mix the blackcurrant purée and sugar syrup together.

4 Transfer the mixture to an ice cream maker and churn until thick. If you are making the sorbet by hand, freeze the mixture in a plastic tub or similar freezerproof container for 4 hours until mushy.

5 Lightly whisk the egg white with a fork until just frothy. If you've used an ice cream maker, just add the egg white and continue to churn until thick enough to scoop. If the mixture was frozen in a tub, soften it by whizzing it briefly in a food processor or blender, then beat in the whisked egg white and return the sorbet to the tub. Freeze for 4 hours, or until firm.

6 Scoop the sorbet into large balls or pare off long shavings into tall glasses and decorate with a sprig of blackcurrants.

COOK'S TIP To pare off long shavings of sorbet, press a dessertspoon into the surface and drag it along at an angle of 45 degrees. Soften the sorbet slightly before making the shavings.

INGREDIENTS

500g|1¼lbs|5 cups blackcurrants, trimmed

350ml|12fl oz|1½ cups water

150g|5oz|⅔ cup caster (superfine) sugar

1 egg white

sprigs of blackcurrants, to decorate

SERVES SIX

iced melon sorbet with pimm's

Freezing sherbet or sorbet in hollowed-out fruit, which is then cut into icy wedges, is an excellent idea. The novel presentation and refreshing flavour make this dessert irresistible on a hot summer afternoon. The idea works particularly well with melon wedges, served on a bed of crushed ice.

1 Put the sugar, honey, lemon juice and water in a pan and heat gently, stirring until the sugar has dissolved. Bring to the boil, then leave to cool.

2 Carefully scoop the melon flesh into a food processor, keeping the shells intact. Set the shells aside.

STEP 2

STEP 5

3 Blend the melon flesh until smooth. Transfer to a bowl, stir in the cooled syrup and chill until very cold. Invert the melon shells and leave them to drain on kitchen paper. Put the shells in the freezer while making the sorbet.

4 Transfer the melon mixture to an ice cream maker and churn until it holds its shape. If you are making the sorbet by hand, pour the mixture into a plastic tub or similar freezerproof container and freeze for 3–4 hours, beating twice with a fork, a whisk or in a food processor, to break up the ice crystals.

5 Pack the sorbet into the melon shells and level the surface with a knife. Use a dessertspoon to scoop out the centre of each filled melon shell to simulate the seed cavity. Cover and freeze overnight until firm.

6 To serve, use a large knife to cut each half into three wedges. Serve on a bed of crushed ice on a large platter or individual serving plates, and decorate with the cucumber slices and borage. Drizzle lightly with Pimm's.

COOK'S TIP If the melon sorbet is too firm to cut when taken straight from the freezer, let it soften in the refrigerator slightly. Take care when slicing the frozen melon shell into wedges. A serrated kitchen knife is easiest to use.

INGREDIENTS

50g|2oz|¼ cup caster (superfine) sugar

30ml|2 tbsp clear honey

15ml|1 tbsp lemon juice

60ml|4 tbsp water

1 cantaloupe or Charentais melon, about 1kg|2¼lb, halved and seeded

crushed ice, cucumber slices and borage leaves, to decorate

Pimm's No. 1, for serving

SERVES SIX

lemon cups with summer fruits

INGREDIENTS

500ml|17fl oz|2¼ cups lemon sorbet

225g|8oz|2 cups small strawberries

150g|5oz|scant 1 cup raspberries

75g|3oz|¾ cup red- or blackcurrants

15ml|1 tbsp caster (superfine) sugar

45ml|3 tbsp Cointreau

SERVES SIX

In this stunning dessert, lemon sorbet is moulded into cup shapes to make pretty containers for a selection of summer fruits. Other combinations, such as lime cups for tropical fruits, or orange cups for blueberries, also work well.

1 Put six 150ml|¼ pint|⅔ cup metal moulds in the freezer for 15 minutes to chill. At the same time, remove the sorbet from the freezer to soften slightly.

2 Using a teaspoon, pack the sorbet into the moulds, about 1cm|½in thick around the base and sides, and leaving a deep cavity in the centre. Hold each mould in a dishtowel as you work. Return each mould to the freezer when it is lined.

3 Cut the small strawberries in half and place in a bowl with the raspberries and redcurrants or blackcurrants. Add the sugar and liqueur and toss the ingredients together lightly. Cover and chill for at least 2 hours.

4 Once the sorbet in the moulds has frozen completely, loosen the edges with a knife, then dip in a bowl of very hot water for 2 seconds. Invert the sorbet cups on to a tray, using a fork to twist and loosen the cups if necessary. Dip the moulds into the hot water again, if they are stuck.

5 Turn the cups over so they are ready to fill and return to the freezer until required.

6 To serve, place the cups on serving plates and fill with the fruits, adding any juices.

COOK'S TIP If you don't have any moulds, use small china ramekin or soufflé dishes lined with clear film (plastic wrap), so that the sorbet can be easily turned out at the end.

iced clementines

These pretty, filled fruits store well in the freezer, and will prove perfect for an impromptu summer party or a lunchtime *al fresco* meal.

1 Slice the tops off 12 of the clementines to make lids. Set them aside on a baking sheet.

2 Loosen the clementine flesh with a sharp knife, then carefully scoop it out into a bowl, keeping the shells intact. Scrape out as much of the membrane from the shells as possible. Rinse and drain the clementine shells well, then add them to the lids and put them in the freezer.

3 Put the sugar and water in a heavy pan and heat gently, stirring until the sugar dissolves. Boil for 3 minutes without stirring, then leave the syrup to cool. Stir in the lemon juice.

4 Finely grate the rind from the remaining four clementines. Squeeze the fruits and add the juice and rind to the syrup.

5 Process the reserved clementine flesh in a food processor or blender, then press it through a sieve placed over a bowl to extract as much juice as possible. Add this to the syrup. You need about 900ml | 1½ pints | 3¾ cups of liquid. Make up with fresh orange juice if necessary.

6 Churn the mixture in an ice cream maker until it holds its shape. If making by hand, pour the mixture into a plastic tub or similar freezerproof container and freeze for 3–4 hours, beating twice as the sherbet thickens. Pack the sorbet into the empty clementine shells, mounding them up in the centre. Position the lids and return to the freezer for several hours or overnight.

7 Transfer the clementines to the refrigerator about 30 minutes before serving, to soften. Serve on individual plates, decorated with mint or lemon balm leaves.

INGREDIENTS

16 large clementines

175g | 6oz | ¾ cup caster (superfine) sugar

105ml | 7 tbsp water

juice of 2 lemons

a little fresh orange juice (if necessary)

fresh mint or lemon balm leaves, to decorate

MAKES TWELVE

chocolate-coffee sherbet

This dark chocolate sherbet is a delicious cross between a water ice and an ice cream. This recipe contains no cream and only semi-skimmed milk, so it makes an ideal treat for chocoholics who are also trying to count calories.

STEP 1   STEP 2

INGREDIENTS

600ml | 1 pint | 2¹/₂ cups
semi-skimmed
(low-fat) milk

40g | 1¹/₂oz | ¹/₃ cup
cocoa powder
(unsweetened)

115g | 4oz | ¹/₂ cup caster
(superfine) sugar

5ml | 1 tsp instant coffee
granules or powder

chocolate-covered raisins,
to decorate

SERVES FOUR TO SIX

1 Heat the milk in a pan until hot, but not boiling. Meanwhile, put the cocoa in a bowl. Add a little of the hot milk to the cocoa and mix to a smooth paste using a wooden spoon. Add the remaining milk to the cocoa mixture, stirring all the time, then pour the chocolate milk back into the pan. Bring to the boil, stirring often.

2 Take the pan off the heat and stir in the sugar and the instant coffee until it has dissolved. Pour into a jug (pitcher), leave to cool, then chill well.

3 Transfer the chilled mixture to an ice cream maker and churn until very thick. If making the sherbet by hand, pour the mixture into a plastic tub or similar freezerproof container and freeze for 6 hours until firm, beating once or twice with a fork. Transfer to a food processor or electric mixer to break up the ice crystals if necessary. Allow the sherbet to soften slightly before serving.

4 Scoop into dishes and sprinkle each portion with a few chocolate-covered raisins.

COOK'S TIP Use good quality cocoa and don't overheat the milk mixture or the finished ice may taste bitter. If there are any lumps of cocoa in the milk, beat the mixture with a balloon whisk to remove them completely.

VARIATION For extra creaminess, add 150ml | ¼ pint | ⅔ cup crème fraîche or softly whipped cream to the cooled sherbet mixture just before freezing.

raspberry sherbet

This modern low-fat sherbet is made from raspberry purée blended with sugar syrup and virtually fat-free fromage frais or cream cheese, then flecked with crushed fresh raspberries.

1 Put the sugar and water in a heavy pan and heat gently, stirring until the sugar has dissolved. Bring to the boil, then pour into a jug (pitcher) and cool.

2 Put 350g | 12oz | 2½ cups of the raspberries in a food processor or blender. Process to a purée, then press through a sieve placed over a large bowl to remove the seeds. Stir the sugar syrup into the raspberry purée and chill the mixture until it is very cold.

3 Add the fromage frais or cream cheese to the purée and whisk until smooth.

4 Transfer the mixture to an ice cream maker and churn until it is thick but not too soft to scoop. Spoon into a freezerproof container. If you are making the sherbet by hand, pour the mixture into a plastic tub or similar freezerproof container and freeze for 4 hours, beating once with a fork, electric whisk or in a food processor to break up the ice crystals. After this time, beat again.

5 Crush the remaining raspberries between your fingers and add them to the partially frozen sherbet. Mix lightly, then freeze for 2–3 hours more until firm.

6 Scoop the sherbet into dishes and serve with extra raspberries.

COOK'S TIP If you intend to make this in an ice cream maker, check your handbook first, as this recipe makes 900ml | 1½ pints | 3¾ cups of mixture. If this is too large a quantity for your machine to handle, make it in two batches or by hand.

INGREDIENTS

175g | 6oz | ¾ cup caster (superfine) sugar

150ml | ¼ pint | ⅔ cup water

500g | 1¼lb | 3½ cups raspberries, plus extra, to serve

500ml | 17fl oz | generous 2 cups virtually fat-free fromage frais or cream cheese

SERVES SIX

STEP 3

STEP 5

water ices

Don't be fooled by the name – water ices may sound as pure as the driven snow, but they often pack a considerable punch. Any recipe that begins with a bottle of red wine, as does the mulled wine ice, is anything but innocent, but there are plenty of alcohol-free alternatives, such as the demure yet delicious damson water ice and the refreshing ginger and kiwi water ice. Turkish delight ice lives up to the promise implied in its title, while frost meets fire in an unusual chilli and lime mixture. Full of flavour, these desserts are real melt-in-the-mouth delights.

damson water ice

These plum-like fruits have a strong, tart flavour which, once cooked with sugar, develops a pleasantly spicy flavour. Use ripe fruits for their natural sweetness. If you can't find damsons, use extra-juicy Victoria plums.

STEP 3   STEP 4

INGREDIENTS

500g | 1¹/₄lb ripe damsons

450ml | ³/₄ pint | scant
2 cups water

150g | 5oz | ²/₃ cup caster
(superfine) sugar

SERVES SIX

1 Put the damsons into a pan and add 150ml | ¼ pint | ²/₃ cup of the water. Cover and simmer for 10 minutes, or until the damsons are tender.

2 Pour the remaining water into a second, heavy pan. Add the sugar and heat gently, stirring occasionally, until all the sugar has all dissolved. Bring to the boil, and cook for a few minutes, then pour the sugar syrup into a small bowl. Set aside to cool completely, then cover and chill.

3 Break up the cooked damsons in the pan with a wooden spoon and scoop out any free stones (pits). Pour the fruit and juices into a large sieve set over a bowl. Press the fruit through the sieve, using the back of a spoon, then discard the skins and any stones remaining in the sieve.

4 Mix the purée with the syrup then transfer to an ice cream maker and churn until firm enough to scoop. If making the water ice by hand, pour the damson purée into a shallow plastic tub or similar freezerproof container. Stir in the syrup and freeze for 6 hours, beating once or twice to break up the ice crystals.

5 Scoop into tall glasses or dishes and serve.

VARIATIONS Apricot water ice can be made in the same way. Flavour the syrup by adding finely sliced lemon or orange rind to the pan containing the water and sugar or add a broken cinnamon stick to the fruit when poaching it.

apple and cider water ice

This classic combination has a subtle apple flavour with just a hint of cider. As the apple purée is very pale, almost white, add a few drops of green food colouring to echo the pale green skin of the Granny Smith apples.

STEP 1

1 Quarter, core and roughly chop the apples. Put them into a small pan. Add the sugar and half the water. Cover the pan and set it over a medium heat. Simmer for 10 minutes, or until the apples are soft and the sugar has all dissolved.

2 Press the mixture through a sieve placed over a bowl. Discard the apple skins and pips (seeds). Stir the cider and the remaining water into the apple purée and add a little colouring, if using.

INGREDIENTS

500g | 1¼lb Granny Smith apples

150g | 5oz | ⅔ cup caster (superfine) sugar

300ml | ½ pint | 1¼ cups water

250ml | 8fl oz | 1 cup strong dry (hard) cider

a few drops of green food colouring (optional)

strips of thinly pared lime rind, to decorate

SERVES SIX

3 Transfer the apple purée to an ice cream maker and churn until firm enough to scoop. If making the water ice by hand, pour the mixture into a shallow plastic tub or similar freezerproof container and freeze for 6 hours, beating with a fork once or twice to break up the ice crystals.

4 Scoop into dishes and decorate with twists of thinly pared lime rind.

COOK'S TIP Add the food colouring gradually, making the mixture a little darker than required as freezing lightens the colour slightly. Add the colouring on the tip of a cocktail stick (toothpick).

VARIATION This water ice is also delicious made with the same weight of ripe, peeled pears or a mixture of apples and pears.

turkish delight water ice

Anyone who likes Turkish delight will adore the taste and aroma of this intriguing dessert. Because of its sweetness, it is best served in small portions and is delicious with after-dinner coffee.

1 Cut the cubes of Turkish delight into small pieces using a pair of kitchen scissors. Put half the pieces in a pan with the sugar. Pour in half the water. Heat gently, until the Turkish delight has completely dissolved.

2 Cool, then stir in the lemon juice with the remaining water and Turkish delight. Chill well.

3 Transfer the mixture to an ice cream maker and churn until it holds its shape. Tip into a freezerproof container and freeze until ready to serve. If making by hand, pour the mixture into a plastic tub or similar freezerproof container and freeze for 3–4 hours, beating twice. Return to the freezer until ready to serve.

4 Meanwhile, dampen eight small freezerproof glasses or plastic cups, then line them with clear film (plastic wrap). Spoon the water ice into the cups or glasses and tap them lightly on the surface to compact the mixture. Cover with the overlapping film and freeze for at least 3 hours or overnight.

5 Just before serving, remove the ices from the freezer, and let them stand at room temperature for 5 minutes. Meanwhile, put the pieces of white chocolate in a heatproof bowl and melt over a pan of gently simmering water.

6 When ready, pull the ices out of the glasses or cups. Invert on to serving plates and peel away the clear film. Spoon the melted chocolate into a piping bag, snip off the tip and scribble a design on the water ice and the plate. Scatter the sugared almonds over and serve.

STEP 1

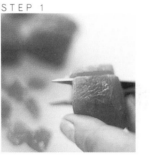

STEP 4

INGREDIENTS

250g | 9oz rose water Turkish delight

25g | 1oz | 2 tbsp caster (superfine) sugar

750ml | 1¹/₄ pints | 3 cups water

30ml | 2 tbsp lemon juice

50g | 2oz white chocolate, broken into pieces

roughly chopped sugared almonds, to decorate

SERVES EIGHT

ginger and kiwi water ice

INGREDIENTS

50g | 2oz fresh root ginger

115g | 4oz | $^1/_2$ cup caster (superfine) sugar

300ml | $^1/_2$ pint | 1$^1/_4$ cups water

5 kiwi fruits

fresh mint sprigs or chopped kiwi fruit, to decorate

SERVES SIX

Freshly grated root ginger gives a lively, aromatic flavour to water ices. Here it is combined with kiwi fruit, which has a delicate yet refreshing and tangy flavour, to make a cleansing and tasty dessert.

1 Peel the ginger and grate it finely. Put the sugar and water in a pan and heat gently until the sugar has dissolved. Add the ginger and cook for 1 minute, then cool. Strain into a bowl, discarding the ginger, and chill.

2 Peel the kiwi fruits and blend in a food processor until smooth. Add the purée to the syrup and mix well.

3 Transfer the mixture to an ice cream maker and churn until it thickens. Spoon into a plastic tub or similar freezerproof container and freeze until ready to serve. If making by hand, pour the mixture into a freezerproof container and freeze for 3–4 hours, beating well twice as it thickens. Return to the freezer until ready to serve.

4 Spoon into glasses, decorate with mint sprigs or chopped kiwi fruit, and serve.

COOK'S TIP For a completely smooth water ice, push the kiwi fruit purée through a fine sieve, to remove the seeds, then stir it into the chilled sugar syrup.

chilli water ice

Served during or after dinner, this unusual but refreshing water ice will become a talking point.

1 Cut the chilli in half, removing all the seeds and any pith with a small sharp knife, then chop the chilli flesh very finely.

2 Put the chilli, lemon and lime rind, sugar and water in a heavy pan. Heat gently and stir while the sugar dissolves. Bring to the boil, then simmer for 2 minutes without stirring. Leave to cool.

3 Add the lemon and lime juice to the chilli syrup and chill until very cold.

4 Transfer the mixture to an ice cream maker and churn until it holds its shape. Spoon into a plastic tub or similar freezerproof container and freeze until ready to serve. If making the water ice by hand, pour the mixture into a shallow freezerproof container and freeze for 3–4 hours, beating twice as it thickens. Return to the freezer until ready to serve.

5 To serve, spoon the water ice into glasses and decorate with citrus rind.

COOK'S TIP Use a medium-hot chilli rather than any of the fiery varieties. Wash your hands thoroughly after preparing the chilli. For an added kick, drizzle the water ice with tequila or vodka before serving.

INGREDIENTS

1 fresh red chilli

finely grated rind and juice of 2 lemons

finely grated rind and juice of 2 limes

225g|8oz|1 cup caster (superfine) sugar

750ml|1$^{1}/_{4}$ pints|3 cups water

pared lemon or lime rind, to decorate

SERVES SIX

mulled wine ice

This dramatic-looking dessert is ideal for serving during the festive season, or any other celebratory occasion. It is spicy and flavoursome, with quite a powerful kick, so is best reserved for adults who won't have to drive home.

INGREDIENTS

1 bottle medium red wine

2 clementines or
1 large orange

16 whole cloves

2 cinnamon sticks, halved

1 apple, roughly chopped

5ml | 1 tsp mixed
(apple pie) spice

75g | 3oz | 1/2 cup light
muscovado
(brown) sugar

150ml | 1/4 pint | 2/3 cup
water

200ml | 7fl oz | scant 1 cup
freshly squeezed
orange juice

45ml | 3 tbsp brandy

pared orange rind,
to decorate

SERVES SIX

STEP 1

STEP 2

1 Pour the bottle of wine into a pan. Gently stud the clementines or orange with the whole cloves, then cut in half. Add to the wine, with the cinnamon sticks, chopped apple, spice, sugar and water. Heat gently, stirring occasionally, until the sugar has dissolved.

2 Cover the pan and cook the mixture gently for 15 minutes. Set aside to cool, then strain into a large bowl. Stir in the orange juice and brandy. Chill until very cold.

3 Transfer the mixture to an ice cream maker and churn until it thickens. Spoon into a plastic tub or similar freezerproof container and freeze until ready to serve. If making the ice by hand, pour the mixture into a freezerproof container and freeze for 3–4 hours, beating twice as it thickens. Return to the freezer until ready to serve.

4 To serve, spoon or scoop into small glasses and decorate with the strips of pared orange rind.

COOK'S TIP You could also serve this ice in clementine shells, if you like. Cut the tops off the fruit, and scoop out all the flesh. Rinse and drain the fruit well before filling. Use the flesh in another recipe.

gooseberry and elderflower water ice

A classic combination that makes a really refreshing dessert. Make it in
summer, when gooseberries and elderflowers are plentiful, and serve it as
a lovely finale for an al fresco meal.

1 Put 30ml|2 tbsp of the sugar
in a pan with 30ml|2 tbsp of
the water. Set aside. Mix the
remaining sugar and water in
a separate, heavy pan. Heat
gently, stirring occasionally,
until the sugar has dissolved.
Bring to the boil and boil for
1 minute, without stirring, to
make a syrup.

STEP 2 STEP 3 STEP 4

2 Remove from the heat and add the elderflower heads, pressing them into the
syrup with a wooden spoon. Leave to infuse for about 1 hour.

3 Strain the elderflower syrup through a sieve placed over a bowl. Set the syrup
aside. Add the gooseberries to the pan containing the reserved sugar and water.
Cover and cook very gently for about 5 minutes until the gooseberries have
softened. Do not let them cook down to a mush.

4 Transfer to a food processor or blender and add the apple juice. Process until
smooth, then press through a sieve into a bowl. Leave to cool. Stir in the
elderflower syrup. Add the green food colouring, if using. Mix well and chill.

5 Transfer the mixture to an ice cream maker and churn until it holds its shape.
Spoon into a plastic tub or similar freezerproof container and freeze for several
hours or overnight. If making by hand, simply pour the mixture into a shallow
freezerproof container and freeze until thick, preferably overnight. Beat once
during freezing.

6 To decorate the serving glasses, put a little egg white in a shallow bowl and a
thin layer of caster sugar on a flat plate. Dip the rim of each glass in the egg
white, then in the sugar to coat evenly. Leave to dry. Scoop the water ice carefully
into the glasses, decorate with the elderflowers and serve.

INGREDIENTS

150g|5oz|⅔ cup caster
(superfine) sugar

175ml|6fl oz|¾ cup water

10 elderflower heads

500g|1¼lb|4 cups
gooseberries

200ml|7fl oz|scant 1 cup
apple juice

a few drops of green food
colouring (optional)

a little beaten egg white,
caster (superfine) sugar
and elderflowers,
to decorate

SERVES SIX

cranberry water ice in lace pancakes

INGREDIENTS

500g/1¼lb/5 cups cranberries

225g/8oz/1 cup caster (superfine) sugar

300ml/½ pint/1¼ cups orange juice

60ml/4 tbsp Cointreau

icing (confectioners') sugar, for dusting

extra cranberries and whipped cream, to serve

Pretty lace pancakes are an elegant way to present this dish. The sweet yet tangy cranberry sorbet can be made using fresh or frozen cranberries and the result is an impressive dinner party dessert at any time of the year.

1 Put the cranberries, sugar and orange juice in a pan; heat gently until the sugar has dissolved. Cover and cook for 5–8 minutes. Set aside to cool, then process the mixture in a food processor or blender until smooth. Press through a sieve placed over a bowl to extract the juice. Stir the liqueur into the juice. Chill.

2 Transfer the mixture into an ice cream maker and churn until the water ice holds its shape. Spoon into a freezerproof container and freeze overnight. If making the water ice by hand, pour the mixture into a shallow tub or similar freezerproof container and freeze for 3–4 hours, beating twice. Freeze overnight.

STEP 3   STEP 4

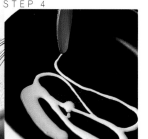

3 Make the pancakes. Sift the flour and ginger into a mixing bowl. Add the egg, sugar and a little of the milk and stir through. Gradually whisk in the remaining milk to make a smooth batter. Heat a little oil in a small frying pan or crêpe pan. Pour off the excess oil and remove the pan from the heat.

FOR THE PANCAKES

50g/2oz/½ cup plain (all-purpose) flour

2.5ml/½ tsp ground ginger

1 egg

15ml/1 tbsp caster (superfine) sugar

120ml/4fl oz/½ cup milk

SERVES SIX

4 Using a dessertspoon, drizzle a little of the batter over the base of the hot pan, using a scribbling action to give a lacy effect. (The pancake should be about 14cm/5½in in diameter.) Return the pan to the heat and cook the mixture gently until the lacy pancake is golden on the underside. Carefully turn it over, and cook for 1 minute more. Slide on to a plate and keep warm. Make five more pancakes in the same way, lightly oiling the pan each time.

5 To serve, lay a pancake on a serving plate. Arrange several small scoops of the water ice on one side of the pancake. Fold over and dust generously with icing sugar. Scatter with extra cranberries and serve with whipped cream.

COOK'S TIP When drizzling the batter into the frying pan, make sure that most of the lacy edges are connected, otherwise the pancakes will fall apart when you try to turn them. Use ready-made pancakes if short of time and warm before using.

granitas

Crystals are said to have magic properties, and there's something undeniably magical in the transformation of black coffee into cool crystals that dissolve on your tongue. Nothing could be simpler than a granita, yet the effect is stunning. Although coffee is the classic choice, the fresh clean taste of citrus or berry fruit works just as well. A little liqueur can be added, but don't overdo it, or the granita won't freeze. Texture is as important as taste in a granita. The secret is frequent whisking with a fork until the ice forms frosty flakes – almost too easy.

coffee granita

This is perhaps the most famous of all granitas. Originating in Mexico, it consists of full-bodied coffee frozen into tiny ice flakes. It is traditionally served in a tumbler with whipped cream on top, but is just as delicious solo.

STEP 1   STEP 2   STEP 3

1 Spoon the coffee into a cafetière (press pot) or tall heatproof jug (pitcher). Pour the water over the coffee. Leave to stand for 5 minutes. Plunge the cafetière or strain the jug. Pour the coffee into a plastic tub or similar container that will fit in your freezer, to a depth of about 2.5cm | 1in.

2 Add the sugar and stir constantly until it has dissolved completely. Leave the mixture to cool, then cover and freeze for 2 hours, or until the coffee mixture around the sides of the container is starting to become mushy.

3 Using a fork, break up the ice crystals and mash the mixture finely. Return the granita to the freezer for 2 hours more, beating every 30 minutes until the ice forms fine, even crystals.

4 After the final beating, return the now slushy granita to the freezer, leaving it for no more than 35–40 minutes. When ready to serve, spoon the granita into glass dishes. Whip the cream and offer it separately, if you like.

COOK'S TIP If you taste the coffee mixture before freezing, don't be alarmed by its strength; the change from liquid to ice mysteriously dulls the flavour, so the finished taste is just right.

INGREDIENTS

75ml | 5 tbsp good quality ground filter coffee

1 litre | 1³/₄ pints | 4 cups very hot water

150g | 5oz | ²/₃ cup caster (superfine) sugar

150ml | ¹/₄ pint | ²/₃ cup double (heavy) cream (optional)

SERVES SIX

raspberry granita

This vibrant bright red granita looks spectacular. Served on its own, it is an excellent, refreshing dessert. For something a little more indulgent, serve with whole berries and crème fraîche or clotted cream, to make an elegant and contemporary dessert in the style of a knickerbocker glory.

STEP 1   STEP 2

STEP 4

1 Put the sugar and water into a heavy pan and heat gently, stirring occasionally until the sugar has all dissolved. Bring to the boil, then pour the sugar syrup into a bowl. Leave to cool, then cover and chill.

2 Purée the raspberries in a food processor or in batches in a blender. Spoon the purée into a fine sieve set over a large bowl. Press the purée through the sieve with the back of the spoon and then discard any remaining seeds.

INGREDIENTS

115g | 4oz | 1/2 cup caster (superfine) sugar

300ml | 1/2 pint | 1 1/4 cups water

500g | 1 1/4lb | 3 1/2 cups raspberries

juice of 1 lemon

SERVES SIX

3 Scrape the purée into a large measuring jug (liquid measure), stir in the sugar syrup and lemon juice and top up to 1 litre | 1¾ pints | 4 cups with cold water. Pour the mixture into a large, shallow plastic tub or a roasting pan that will fit in your freezer, to a depth of not more than 2.5cm | 1in. Cover and freeze for about 2 hours until the mixture around the sides of the container is mushy.

4 Using a fork, break up the ice crystals and mash finely. Return to the freezer for 2 hours, beating every 30 minutes until the ice forms fine, even crystals.

5 Spoon into dessert glasses or dishes and serve.

COOK'S TIP For a granita with a little extra oomph, stir in 45ml | 3 tbsp crème de cassis, but don't be tempted to add more or the granita will not freeze. If you miss one of the beatings, don't panic. Leave the granita at room temperature for about 15 minutes to soften, then beat thoroughly with a fork until it is the required consistency. Return it to the freezer and continue with the recipe.

watermelon granita

This pastel pink granita owes its colour and delicate flavour to watermelon, which has been subtly blended with the citrus freshness of lime. On a hot summer's afternoon it will appeal to young and old alike.

1 Put the sugar and water in a pan, heat, then bring to the boil. Pour into a heatproof bowl. Cool, then chill.

2 Cut the watermelon into quarters. Discard most of the seeds, scoop the flesh into a food processor and process briefly until smooth.

STEP 3

STEP 4

STEP 2

3 Strain the purée into a large shallow plastic tub or a roasting pan that will fit in your freezer. Discard the seeds in the sieve. Pour the chilled syrup into the tub or pan, add the lime rind and juice and mix well. Cover and freeze for 2 hours until the mixture around the sides of the container is mushy. Mash the ice finely with a fork and return the granita to the freezer.

4 Freeze for 2 hours more, mashing the mixture every 30 minutes, until the granita has a fine slushy consistency. Scoop it into dishes and serve with lime wedges for squeezing over.

VARIATION To serve this granita cocktail-style, dip the rim of each glass serving dish in a little water or beaten egg white, then dip it into sugar. Carefully spoon in the granita, pour over a little Cointreau, tequila or white rum and decorate with lime wedges or thin strips of lime rind removed with a cannelle knife (zester) and twisted around a cocktail stick (toothpick).

INGREDIENTS

150g | 5oz | $^2/_3$ cup caster (superfine) sugar

150ml | $^1/_4$ pint | $^2/_3$ cup water

1 whole watermelon, about 1.75kg | 4–4$^1/_2$lb

finely grated rind and juice of 2 limes

lime wedges, to serve

SERVES SIX

ruby grapefruit granita

INGREDIENTS

200g | 7oz | scant 1 cup
caster (superfine) sugar

300ml | 1/2 pint | 1 1/4 cups
water

4 ruby grapefruit

tiny fresh mint leaves,
to decorate

SERVES SIX

This is slightly sharper than the other granitas, but is very refreshing. It's the ideal choice for serving after a rich or very filling main course. Look out for other varieties of grapefruit, such as the green-skinned pomelo.

1 Put the sugar and water into a pan. Heat gently, stirring occasionally until the sugar has dissolved, then bring to the boil. Pour the syrup into a heatproof bowl, cool, then chill.

2 Cut the grapefruit in half. Squeeze the juice, taking care not to damage the grapefruit shells. Set these aside. Strain the juice into a large shallow plastic tub or a roasting pan that will fit in your freezer. Discard any seeds. Add the syrup to the juice, to a depth of no more than 2.5cm | 1in, stirring well.

3 Cover and freeze for 2 hours, or until the mixture around the sides of the tub is mushy. Using a fork, break up the ice crystals and mash the granita finely. Return the tub to the freezer.

4 Freeze for 2 hours more, mashing the mixture every 30 minutes until the granita consists of a mass of fine, even crystals.

5 Select the six best grapefruit shells to use as serving dishes. Using a sharp knife, remove the grapefruit pulp, leaving the shells as clean as possible. Rinse and drain before using.

6 Scoop the granita into the grapefruit shells, decorate with tiny mint leaves and serve.

COOK'S TIP Grapefruit shells make very good serving dishes. For a more modern treatment, consider the effect you would like to achieve with the grapefruit. They look great when tilted at an angle. Having squeezed the juice and removed the membrane, trim a little off the base of each shell so that it will remain stable when filled with granita.

star anise granita

This refreshing dessert will grab attention as it is both tangy and sweet. The dramatic appearance of star anise makes it an ideal decoration.

1 Put the sugar and water in a pan and heat gently, stirring occasionally, until the sugar has completely dissolved. Bring to the boil, then add the star anise and heat the syrup for 2 minutes, without stirring. Remove the syrup from the heat and leave to cool.

2 Peel the grapefruit, then chop the flesh roughly, discarding the pips (seeds). Place the flesh in a food processor or blender. Process until almost smooth, then press the pulp through a sieve into a bowl.

3 Strain the syrup into the bowl, reserving the star anise. Mix well, then pour the mixture into a shallow plastic tub or a roasting pan that will fit in your freezer, making sure it comes to a depth of no more than 2.5cm | 1in. Cover and freeze for 2 hours, or until the mixture starts to freeze and form ice crystals around the edges of the container.

4 Using a fork, break up the ice crystals, then return the mixture to the freezer. Freeze for a further 30 minutes, mash lightly with a fork again, then return to the freezer. Repeat the process until the granita consists of a mass of very fine, even ice crystals.

5 To serve, spoon the granita into tall glasses or bowls and decorate with the reserved star anise.

COOK'S TIP Buy whole star anise from a shop or market that sells spices loose or packaged in clear Cellophane. When the spice is packed in boxes, it is often broken into sections and the quality and flavour will have deteriorated.

INGREDIENTS

200g | 7oz | scant 1 cup caster (superfine) sugar

450ml | 3/4 pint | scant 2 cups water

6 whole star anise

4 grapefruit

SERVES SIX

tequila and orange granita

INGREDIENTS

115g | 4oz | ½ cup caster
(superfine) sugar

200ml | 7fl oz | scant 1 cup
water

6 oranges, well scrubbed

90ml | 6 tbsp tequila

orange and lime wedges,
to decorate

SERVES SIX

Full of flavour, this distinctive Mexican granita will have guests clamouring for more. Serve simply with wedges of citrus fruit or spoon over a little grenadine for a rosy glow reminiscent of a tequila sunrise.

1 Put the sugar and water into a pan. Using a vegetable peeler, thinly pare the rind from three of the oranges, letting it fall into the pan. Heat gently, stirring until the sugar has completely dissolved. Bring to the boil, then pour the syrup into a heatproof bowl, cool, then chill.

2 Strain the syrup into a shallow plastic tub or a roasting pan that will fit in your freezer. Squeeze all the oranges, strain the juice into the syrup, then stir in the tequila. Check that the mixture is no more than 2.5cm | 1in deep; transfer to a larger container if necessary.

3 Cover and freeze for 2 hours until the mixture around the sides of the container is mushy. Mash well with a fork and return the granita to the freezer.

4 Freeze for 2 hours more, mashing the mixture with a fork every 30 minutes until the granita has a fine slushy consistency.

5 Scoop it into dishes and serve with the orange and lime wedges.

COOK'S TIP If you don't have any tequila, make the granita with vodka, Cointreau or even white rum. Don't be tempted to add more than the recommended amount; too much alcohol will stop the granita from freezing.

VARIATION For a fun, long, cool drink, scoop the granita into tall glasses, add a splash of orange or lime juice and top up with fizzy lemonade.

STEP 1

STEP 2

peach and almond granita

Infused almonds make a richly flavoured "milk" that forms the basis of this light, tangy dessert. It would be the ideal choice to follow a spicy curry or a rich main course. The liqueur adds a subtle mellowness to the dish.

1 Put the ground almonds in a pan and pour in 600ml | 1 pint | 2½ cups of the water. Bring just to the boil, then lower the heat and simmer for 2 minutes. Remove from the heat and leave to stand for 30 minutes.

2 Strain the mixture through a fine sieve placed over a bowl, and press lightly with the back of a spoon, to extract as much liquid as possible. Pour the liquid into a clean pan and stir in the sugar and almond essence, with half the lemon juice and the remaining water.

3 Heat gently until the sugar dissolves, then bring to the boil. Lower the heat and simmer gently for 3 minutes without stirring, taking care that the syrup does not boil over. Remove from the heat and leave to cool.

4 Cut the peaches in half and remove the stones (pits). Scoop out about half the flesh from each peach to enlarge the cavities. Put the flesh in a food processor or blender. Lightly brush the exposed flesh of the peach halves with the remaining lemon juice and chill them until required.

5 Add the almond syrup to the peach flesh in the processor and blend until smooth. Pour into a shallow tub or similar freezerproof container and freeze until ice crystals have formed around the edges. Stir with a fork, then freeze again until more crystals have formed around the edges. Repeat until the mixture has the consistency of crushed ice.

6 To serve, lightly break up the granita with a fork to loosen the mixture. Spoon into the peach halves and serve two on each plate. Drizzle a little amaretto liqueur over the top of each filled peach half, if you like.

COOK'S TIP The scooped peach shells will keep overnight in the refrigerator if you brush them with lemon juice and wrap them in clear film (plastic wrap). If you want to make the dessert further ahead, simply use the flesh of three peaches for the granita and serve in tall glasses instead of the peach shells.

INGREDIENTS

115g | 4oz | 1 cup ground almonds

900ml | 1½ pints | 3¾ cups water

150g | 5oz | ⅔ cup caster (superfine) sugar

5ml | 1 tsp almond essence (extract)

juice of 2 lemons

6 peaches

amaretto liqueur, to serve (optional)

SERVES SIX

index